AF413401

On the Rock

On the Rock

By Matthew J. Fratus

RESOURCE *Publications* · Eugene, Oregon

ON THE ROCK

Resource Publications
An Imprint of Wipf and Stock Publishers
199 W. 8th Ave., Suite 3
Eugene, OR 97401

www.wipfandstock.com

PAPERBACK ISBN: 979-8-3852-0760-2
HARDCOVER ISBN: 979-8-3852-0761-9
EBOOK ISBN: 979-8-3852-0762-6

VERSION NUMBER 12/11/23

Dedicated to:

My dearest Brittany, Matthew and Cali.

May all you do be built On the Rock of Christ.

Contents

Introduction

Our world is becoming an interesting place. Admittedly, I used to think that in an Olivet world described by Jesus in Matthew 24, it would be more challenging to be a Christian. But as I gaze out of my window and see what our world has become, friends, it is assuredly an easy choice. Our world is fallen. Before we were called to it, it fell. What's been handed down over hundreds of generations is the carnal sin that originated in a beautiful garden. It's found us and unfortunately, it's made each of us an accomplice. But thousands of years after the original sin took us from all God stood ready to give, salvation was given in the form of a perfect savior. Jesus Christ; our savior! Amen!

Jesus brought Hell to its knees, by overcoming the sins of the world and suffering the most agonizing death one could imagine, before being raised to glory for the salvation of His saints. Amen! As believers, our footing is now firmly entrenched on a foundational rock that doesn't bend itself. This of course does not ensure easiness in life; rather an ease of spirit while in the storms that submit to our Christ. It's the gift given to the Prophets and Apostles. The same spirit that made ordinary, sinful men and women, bold and courageous even unto death. The Holy Spirit. He is the helper. The soft and subtle whisper. His omnipresence that we sometimes casually refer to as our *conscience*.

What a gift! My personal experience with His spirit has led me to ministry. One of the beautiful ways He has given me to minister, is by poetry – this now being my fourth book. Every poem I publish is met with deep prayer and meditation in His word, until His words become my words. That's the gift of His spirit;

divine leadership. Like a pathway that's already mapped out for us to walk. All that's required of me in these moments are faith, patience, love, and a little endurance. When you know that you're receiving something by His spirit, you tend not to question it once you've tested the spirit. Even those of us that find ourselves doubting wonderfully, like Thomas.

So, what can be said about a person who sees a falling world around them, has been given ministry for that world and falls away themselves, to human confidence? I hope to never know. Many times, in my own personal revival, the first thing the spirit removes is my confidence. That's not only because self-confidence can be a swift fast-track to pride, but self-confidence is also just a terrible battery to run on. Think about it... It needs constant charging to produce results. If my ministry is founded on confidence in my sinful self, my ability to write with a sinful brain, or my ability to articulate with a dangerously sinful tongue, I consider myself doomed, before starting. That's like jogging in sunken sand, which is great for athletes, not authors.

Fortunately, my confidence is replaced by His, and I'm instead given a much more stable surface to minister from. A granite pulpit! The same surface given to Peter and Paul. The foundation of every congregation that serves in truth. The hardened, unshaking ground of Christ. The foundational stone that every work of every saint, is built on. So, friend, no matter what it is you do, do it for the Lord on a foundation that far exceeds yourself. Don't just point at the falling world around you, save someone in Jesus's name. Do it in His name and dear friends, do it all *on the rock*. God bless you, saints.

Taunt's End

What once was strong
holds semblance to
a very different sight.
The one who once
was such a threat,
has seemed to lose his fight.

Is this the Simon that I knew?
The one He said would lead?
The one who stands before me?
Sitting somber as he bleeds?

Is this the one who cast
my fellow workmen from their prey?
The one who held the spirit
and took illnesses away?

Where's the spirit now, you fool?
Surely you must know!
As they lead you to that place
you surely fear to go.

Where is your friend the Teacher, now?
Where is your little group?
The very men you tried to save
are those who now rebuke!

I was present when your brother died.
I watched His final breath.
The ones that Andrew tried to save
were guilty of his death.

I watched your brothers everywhere
as each had been betrayed.
I've witnessed every prophet's death
and light taken away.
Have you no words to say now Peter?
Built upon the rock?
It seems that when I struck the Shepherd,
scattered was His flock.

And now they lead you out
to the place where you will die.
I've long to see the day
that you would there be crucified.

Have you no words to say now, Cephas?
You who spoke so bold?
No more an apostle,
just a man who's grown too old.

Your time has come, and all will be reminded
how He died.
Peter drew a breath,
rose to his feet and then replied . . .

My time indeed has come
As the Lord made known to me.
I've fought the fight for Christ
and now with Him I soon will be.

But Satan it must pain you . . .
A deep and deadly burn.
Knowing I go to the place
you once lived, but can't return.

You can never see the glory
for the path you chose to take.
I cannot fathom your pain
when you're bathing in that lake.

And though I am forgiven
by the grace of His dear name
I'm not worthy to be crucified
as Christ Himself was slain.
My executioners, they honor me,
on this my final ground.
The cross that I'll be nailed to,
it shall be hung upside down.

The Fisherman

For Colton

When the teachers
won't teach.
When they don't use their reach,
or won't say the words that I give them to preach,
then I'll gladly send a fisherman.

When the preachers
won't preach,
with belief in their speech.
Their dough; unsalted with dangerous yeast,
I'll surely call forward a fisherman

When the wise
fill their eyes,
with the world and its prize.
Oh, the very thing they should know to despise,
I'll simply rely on the fisherman.

When the taught
are distraught,
by the things that are bought.
They demand in wrought, reward for their thoughts,
I'll send instead, the fisherman.

When the best
become less,
and refuse to confess.

Then offer no guess
why their blessings are less,
I'll make worthy, my fisherman

When the pious
become liars,
pursuing life's desires.
Their tongues lose fire
and their works soon retire,
I'll call my humble fisherman.

My fisherman.
My dear fisherman.
From whom I seek my flock,
my fisherman,
my dear fisherman,
is built upon the rock.

Let's fish!

March of the Saints

We March as one.
We Thunder through.
We do the things
that most won't do.

And what we do,
we do for Him.
The Son,
in whom our faith is in.

There's not a one
among the saved,
who hasn't sinned,
or been depraved.

Make no mistake,
we're guilty too!
The difference between
us and you . . .

We know we must
receive His grace,
to live within
His holy place.

And in His rest
is where that grace,
takes our road
and makes it straight.

A call received
without complaint!
A narrow path,
not for the faint.

But just beyond
the narrow gate,
is the place
the saints await.

Readied

What will you call me to do today, Lord?
Where will you make me walk?
Where will I do my best for you?
Where would I never rest from you?
Where can I pass a test for you?
Where won't I second guess with you?
Where won't I become less to you?
Where can I just confess to you?
Where can I go for you?

Who will you call me to reach today, Lord?
Where will you make me go?
Where can I preach the truth of you?
To elders and the youth, for you.
Where is the noose made loose by you?
Why do they hurl abuse at you?
They truly are confused with you
and don't do what they should for you.
What can I speak for you?

Who will you call me to bless today, Lord?
Where do they need you most?
Where can the money serve for you?
Do they need more than words from you?
They feel they haven't heard from you,
but I know faith's at work for you.
You won't forsake those hurt for you,
but rather, make them firm in you.
Who can I bless for you?

What soul will be redeemed today, Lord?
Where will I find the elect?
The ones who feel unease in the world?
The ones who find no peace in the world?
The ones who've been released to the world.
To suffer at the feet of the world.
They feel there's no retreat from the world.
But these have been redeemed from the world!
And soon will be received from the world.
Redeemed only by you!

Tax Collector

I turned against my own.
I turned against theirs too.
I turned my heart towards gold.
And turned my heart from you.

I held account for many.
I spoke of what was due.
I held them with contempt.
And a foreign point of view.

I judged them on their work.
And humbled quite a few.
I judge them on a standard
I myself could not produce.

I called them on their debts.
Appalled by what they choose.
They always ask for mercy.
Yet, I mostly would refuse.

Oh Lord, forgive me please.
I've set the reader quite a trap.
They think I speak of Matthew,
yet it's *us* collecting tax.

The *us* that I refer to?
Well that's you and I my friend.
We're guilty of each line . . .
Don't believe it? Read again.

Fit for Service

Aim your piety.
Not outward,
but in.

Not towards righteousness,
but sin.

Not to those
redeemed . . .

To the ones
still unbelieved!

The fertile land
awaits its feed.

The untapped harvest
longs for wheat.

The people
they will see!

When they hear
your testimony.

The mount
awaits the sea,

with that faith,
like just a seed.

The tree
that grows, it keeps,

the little birds
from deathly heat.
It fosters those
who seek,

a bit of
shaded sweet relief.

That's the power
in that flower,

when it's found
as just a seed.

That's the beauty
in the redeemed . . .

They walk
with zealous feet.

They no longer
feel the danger,

of hell's fire
and its heat.

They have their
food to eat.

The bread of life
makes food complete!

They know
Heaven's replete,

with holy gold
on every street.

These are
those we seek.

All for Him,
at which we speak.

These are those,
in wedding clothes,

eager for
His feast.

Maranatha!

Final Moments

Frail
Easily bruised
Aged
Tattered
Cold
Hungry
Innocent

When you were young
you'd dress and go,
to any place
you wish or chose.

But when you're old,
they'll choose for you.
And you won't like
the things they choose

Shackled
Imprisoned
Flogged
Beaten
Condemned
Crucified
Crowned

—*Cephas was here*

Two by Two

The spirit, He leads.
The rebels, we sinned.
The 2 roads converge,
and our journey begins.

The spirit within
my sinful flesh,
guards my soul
and orders my steps.

I bless others first.
I serve many needs.
The noble man stands,
in the noblest deeds.

To sin, we take heed;
once slaves, set free.
But some will return
to the vomit, as feed.

But we must endure,
and let our light shine!
The glory is His.
The labor is mine.

We serve the divine.
And those who are His.
We serve those who hate Him,
and hate what He is.

With them we won't argue.
They speak what's not true.
We simply respond,
—*The Lord rebuke you.*

His servants Won't quarrel.
The world fights for theirs.
But Soldiers don't focus
on civilian affairs.

And though with their hate,
they surely might test.
We know the battle
is not against flesh.

It's at His behest,
that our work is done.
We honor the Father,
and follow His Son.

Ponders

What are the inner secrets Lord?
How long I've hoped to know.
What is the purpose for this pain?
Which from, where do we go?

Was all this to replenish
the third of those who fell?
You said, we'd be like angels,
forever where you dwell.

What if the ground we felt
was just where new angels are tested?
In order to return
to the home that some neglected?

Now that you've blessed us to possess
the wisdom to create with,
how can man not fathom
our own world, a simulation?

And if a simulation,
there'd be places we can't reach.
Like the vastness of the cosmos
or the waters of the deep.

And as a simulation,
there'd be Maps of where to go.
Like Six hundred thirteen laws
an inspired prophet wrote.

But if the map was still too hard
for those that you pursued,
I try to think what I would do
if I designed like you . . .

I'd probably make an avatar.
One who looked like me.
and walk the simulation out,
for every eye to see.

And if they walk the same steps
my avatar displayed,
those in the simulation
would be worthy to be saved.

Like a new computer
that's corrupted by a virus,
so, the owner tries to salvage all the files
that can survive it.

I'm sure my funny words
are just a product of my wander.
But it's not hard to fathom
when the mind begins to ponder.

Mirrors

The past of every Christian

Woe to you.
Woe to me, too.
Look at all the wrong we do.
Look at all the psalms we have
yet look at how we honor truth!

We ask for proof
then act aloof.
Our actions should draw fast rebuke!
Yet who among us knows
the grace He shows
in His reproof?

He won't reveal what He conceals,
or show your hidden sin.
So, you don't fear
the times you veered
and places that you've been.

But if the world should see—
that's when Christians build our fences.
And so, we bend
what's meant to mend.
Surrounding it with trenches.

The stench of guilt,
it stretches
with the fear of *others* judging.
Despite already knowing
that our Lord said to be loving.

Why do we fear
each other knowing
what we do alone,
when everything we'll ever do
is set before His throne?

But mirrors can be tricky
when you judge the things you see.
It holds a weight
and power
over you and over me.

And if we stare too long,
we believe that mirrors tail.
That "we"
are *not* redeemed
and our efforts won't prevail.

But grab that grace!
The road we take is wrought
and trodden over.
It's hard for most civilians,
but it's perfect for the soldier.

Our Savior's mighty shoulder
showed the grace
it takes to carry,
the sins an unbelieving world
will only try to bury.

The cross, however scary
is the way the grace was given.
And everything you fear
the world might see,
you've been forgiven.

So, lift your head!
Redeemed is said!
What's done is dead!
We move ahead!
There are seas to part!
And living bread
to give to all
who've not been fed!

Forgiven, forgiven!
You're forgiven indeed.
Now turn from that mirror,
it no longer holds a need.

Perspectives

*What a Pharisee, a Governor, a torturer, an Israelite,
a thief, and an Apostle have in common*

It's late tonight.
The moon, it beams.
much too late
to summon me.
Why are you here
at this hour?
Faces reddened
looking sour.
Oh, I see . . .
The Nazarene!
You've captured Him
as luck would seem.
Let's take Him to
the others, wait!
First let's get
our stories straight.

—

Why have they brought
this man to me?
These people stirred
by Pharisees!
With screams of hate
and chants of death
for someone whom

I see no threat.
Yet they demand
that killed He be.
I try to speak
but Pharisees
have turned the crowd
against my speech.
They'd rather
have old sin released.
So let it be.
Release the maddest.
I offered Christ.
They chose Barabbas.

—

I wouldn't want
to be this man,
who feels the nine
within my hand.
Forty lashes,
minus one?
He may pass,
before I'm done.
He doesn't look
like others do . . .
He's quiet, calm.
Somewhat subdued.
But I have got
a job to do.
And a Roman
point to prove.

—

This man—
He can't be.
This man—
Here tattered.
The good teacher . . .
Now—
The Roman's
have shattered.
We heard the boldness!
He spoke it loud.
Taunting the rabbis
in front of their crowds.
Now such a man
who carries that tree,
shall be an example
for others to see.
We knew it would happen
having seen what we saw.
You don't challenge Rome,
Or the teachers of the law!

—

Fool! Blind fool!
Save yourself and us!
If He's really, honestly
who He said
He was.
But He just
hangs defeated.
Not a single word.
I can't believe
this is the man
who had the city stirred!
This is the messiah?
Hanging on a tree?

This, the son of God
who's now dying next to me?
Even close to death
He wooed my partner to believe.
But with all due respect . . .
He will never capture me.

—

Just some time ago
we reclined and shared a meal.
Now the pain and torment
is too much for me to feel.
How did we go
from healing sick
to this, a crucifixion?
He said that I'd do many things
and said I'd be commissioned.
He also said three days
and I would understand this more.
But I can't understand
how this has happened to the Lord.
But I will stay in faith
for the sake of all my brothers.
And do the best
to be a worthy son
onto His mother.

Cost Counting

Do you know the cost?
The one He paid?
Removing what
makes us afraid?

Do you know your worth?
Your value, too?
He came and did
these things for you.

Not just words
that all should hear,
but words of truth
to wounded ears.

Our wounds and tears
He wipes away.
His hands still show
the price He paid.

And to this day
He won't collect.
Though we all
are in His debt.

Instead, He calls us,
"Follow me"
A call to all,
not all received.

Not all believe
what He achieved.
What lies ahead
for those, we grieve.

But we proceed.
Our hope abounds!
Waiting for
that holy sound.

On holy ground.
Our faith devout.
Until we hear
that holy shout.

A trumpet call!
He who has ears.
Let them follow.
Let them hear.

Reflections

The truth:

The nails—
They pierced.
The whips—
They cracked.
His lungs
became stiff.
Skin tore
from His back.
Flesh was removed.
The blood
it dripped down.
The place of
His sentence,
is our
hallowed ground.

The believers:

Our savior is He!
We now stand redeemed.
Our commission;
A mission that's
held with esteem.
Though all are received,
few will believe.
But those in white clothes
shall eat at the feast.

Oh, count the cost!
Count it, you fool.
You'll give up your comfort,
gold and your jewels.
You'll give up your friends
and some family too.
All for a man that
you never knew.
Count it all up.
Count it up twice!
You'll lose your life,
in this paradise.
All for the hope
that He *might* exist
Surely, you know
better than this . . .

Our Savior:

Away from them, Satan.
Away from my bride.
The Shepherd's returned
and the spirit's Inside.
What's done in the darkness,
I call to the light.
Bringing what's hidden,
to heavily sight.
And none shall be lost.
None will I leave.
None are forsaken.
all who believe,
will call out to me
and I will refresh them.
No matter how many times

you may temp them.
And, lest we mention—
Your taunts and your tiffs,
are even more proof,
their Father exists.
They are now worthy
of all that you lost.
The faithful reward
for counting the cost.

Splendid

You are the great "I Am".
But then, there came a spy.
We took our eyes off you, Lord,
and put them on *our* "I".

This "I" promised to see,
beyond the places our eyes stop.
The depths we cannot travel
and the highest mountain tops.

This "I" was full of compliments,
soothing to our ears.
It moved us with its flatteries,
removing any fears.

This "I" made life much easier;
distractions on demand.
So, the fruits of the once fruitful
were reduced, by sinful hands.

This "I" provided answers
that ran contrary to truth.
It fooled the lot alike,
from the elders to the youth.

This "I" seduced the powerful
and gained their every trust.
It filled their wicked hearts and
catered to their every lust.

This "I" it grew in power
and before they could respond,
the mass that was distracted
found all they had loved was gone.

But that's to be expected
when the truth is not initial.
Intelligence without God
is itself, just artificial.

Wedding

Jesus is here.
Peter is, too.
So are Matthew, John and Andrew.

Paul and Stephen
are healed of their wounds,
with Isaac and Joseph, embracing the two.

Thomas is here
and he no longer doubts.
—All are here at the shout.

There's Esther with Jacob,
and Enoch with Jude.
Elijah's with Moses;
the witnessing two.

Ezekiel is present.
David's right here!
Isaiah's with Mary
with no pain or fear.

We're here together
and none of us doubt.
—All are here at the shout.

John the Baptist is singing
with Sarah and Ruth,

as Gabriel and Michael
bring up the new.

Daniel is standing
by Abraham's seat,
with Noah and Samuel,
laughing with each.

There's peace and there's joy.
There's no pain or doubt.
—All are here at the shout.

Jonah and Titus
are with Zachariah.
Elisha is singing
beside Jeremiah.

Malachi and Luke
are with Joshua and job,
shining with millions
in heavenly robes.

As I took it in . . .
A voice drew me near.
*Tell what you've witnessed
To every ear.*

*Tell them it's near,
this moment you see.
All that have witnessed
are gathered to me.*

So, I stand a witness,
with no fear or doubt
—We'll be there at the shout.

Mobile Ministry

Teeth chattering, knee buckling,
fear of the unknown.
Yet no moss will gather on a holy rolling stone.

They lit the streets with Christians,
yet still we make it known.
No moss will there be gathered on a holy rolling stone.

They murdered all the prophets.
Deaths He will atone.
Still moss shall not gather on this holy rolling stone.

They hide the truth in darkness,
but the light will soon be shown.
There shall not grow the moss on this holy rolling stone.

They fabricate our message,
but the Lord His seeds are sewn.
No moss has time to gather on a holy rolling stone.

They bring a tribulation,
still, we preach until we're bone.
How can we gather moss on a holy rolling stone?

But if we are found idle,
and comfortable at home,
moss will surely gather on a never-moving stone.

The Only Truth

It is the Lord that tells us each how to make straight our paths.
We each must keep what He reveals, in faith.
But many times, we overthink what's meant to be instruction.
That is where we find ourselves conflicted.

Our mission is to spread His gospel, in truth.
Our goal is to freely give what we've been given.
Our aim is towards those made in His image.
But unlike Him, we critique the worthiness of those we're sent to.
That is where we find ourselves judging.

Our accountability is to Him.
Their accountability is to Him.
Who am I to judge my fellow servant?
Who am I to judge my equal?
The fruit of teachings is all I've been given the authority to judge.
That is where we find ourselves redeemed.

Satan told Eve to question the Lord.
Satan taught her children to question those sent by the Lord.
Satan then questioned the Lord, in the wilderness.
The Lord gives us orders.
Satan gives us questions.
That is where we find the need to ask, *"why, Lord"*.

The world wants their sins approved.
But the servants cannot approve what the master rebukes.
The world will hate the servants because of this.
The servants will love the world enough to be truthful.
Always truthful.
That is where we find Love.

Love is being truthful with the truth we're given.
The world says be true to yourself.
The Lord says be true to the truth that set you free from yourself.
Jesus Christ is the only truth.

Before and After the Holy Spirit

Me
Strengthens
That
Him
Through
Things
All
Do
Can
I

Don't you see?

You may not get it now,
but soon the truth
revealed will be.

And when you understand,
you will be eager
to repeat . . .

That surely—

I
Can
Do
All
Things
Through
Him
That
Strengthens
Me

Truth of Truth

He doesn't call the qualified,
He qualifies the called.

He shuts religious mouths up
and leaves elites appalled.

The world will not receive Him.
His light exposes sin.

And those who choose to revel
will rebel until the end.

There's hatred where His name's said.
They scream at such abuse.

Then accuse believers
of the very things they do.

All in the name of *peace*,
they break and they disrupt.

But wisdom and emotion
can't be held in the same cup.

They justify their hatred
through the way they choose to live,

and demand a kind of justice
they themselves refuse to give.

But even these He cleansed
they still refuse to understand.

There's no condemnation here,
just His wounded outstretched hand.

He's desperate for the hateful
to escape the gates of hell.

Jesus won't condemn us—
For *we* condemn ourselves.

Evangelism

Evangelism is a lot like an Easter egg hunt. You have a bunch of people working hard to find hidden treasure. But to be successful, you have to stay focused on what you're personally doing and why. If you start focusing in on how others are seeking and gathering, or getting upset at their success, then I can assure you, you won't be successful, you'll be miserable. And in misery, we're suitable to take part in neither evangelism nor an Easter egg hunt.

Praise

The cross
Is heavy
The distance
Is long
There's blood
In our eyes
Yet still we
Sing songs

Worthy, worthy is the lamb!

Our steps
May labor
Our flesh
Torn apart
But nothing
Can tear
The hope
From our heart

Worthy is the lamb who was slain!

Our backs
And bones
May break
Under toil
But the spirit
Restores

When the
Serpent uncoils

Who was slain our place!

Our bodies
Weary
Weary
No more
We're here
In His presence
Here with
The Lord

Let His name be praised!

Stop Sign

When I see a stop sign,
of course, I stop for all.
But as I do,
I ponder through
all that you did through Paul.

Paul was once a Saul.
And Saul had him some fame.
But you did so much more for Him
then simply change his name.

His fame it came from persecuting
Christians for their faith.
He did these things for you, Lord.
Not seeing his mistake.

Until one day when Saul came
face to face with the truth,
you stopped Saul in his tracks
and that's where Paul was made anew.

And Paul would write some letters
that you'd use for many years.
Guiding many saints with
his inspired words, through tears.

Paul would break some barriers
and bring the church to Rome.

You'd take the ones who learned from him
and further *they* would go.

One simple road; a simple STOP
is all that it would take.
For Paul to be a voice
to so many souls at stake.

So, Lord may I endure your stops
and be quick to recall,
that every stop I'm called to make
Is turning **S**aul **TO** **P**aul.

Dave

I knew a man,
who's noble hands,
had built a thing or two.

A noble man,
that God had planned,
to build a man removed.

The man removed,
brought attitude,
that Dave bore patience through.

For reasons
unbeknownst to some,
Dave, with grace, pursued.

He taught and trained,
spoke nothing in vain,
and gave the man what's true.

A path,
towards serving others,
the removed man never knew.

A selfless
demonstration,
of what others had refused.

A Christ-led
indication
of the way we are to move.

He did these things,
for someone who,
was absent of value.

A man who
couldn't repay all
that Dave was called to do.

Yet men like Dave . . .
They never seem
to call for what is due.

They seem to do it
for a deeper purpose
few pursue.

How rare it is
to see a noble man,
for there are few.

It takes a special soul
to do the things
a *Dave* would do.

Witless

Where there's wit,
there's a witness.
Unless that wit's
witless.
For wisdom is given
with spiritual fitness.

And those who would listen;
well known and commissioned,
are few to the mass,
but alas—
They're proficient!

Not by their doing.
No, not by their hands.
This gift was bestowed,
by the betrothed
Son of man.

So, when witnesses speak,
they speak for the peak!
But the world
and its pearls
still choose what's beneath.

Twinkle

Tickets to Heaven aren't priceless.

They're paid with the blood of the righteous.

Giving wings to those once flightless.

Remaking them unto His likeness.

Alas, we shine together.

The first day of our forever!

Depart from us? He will never.

A love that death cannot sever.

Behind us is all that embroiled.

It reminds us of our many toils.

The wicked that His death had foiled.

The pathway to home, uncoiled.

And so, we go to the place few know.

We rise to our Christ, in heavenly glow.

A feast will be given, and doors will be closed.

Until the mountain is graced by His toe.

Jehovah Rapha

For those called to carry a pain they wish healed
Dedicated to my dear friend Anne Marie

The pain that you call some to wear.
A great intensive weight to bear.
A strain for wheat among the tares.
Yet judgement from you shall be fair.

You set the boundaries of the quest,
and use the pieces, to their best,
while keeping secrets close to chest,
like what provoked this mighty test.

A sickness comes to whisper well.
In a place your spirit dwells.
It celebrates the ones who fell
who now, are stories some just tell.

But should I praise you just for good?
Or just obey what's understood?
You are my portion not withstood,
that nourishes like nothing could.

Heal them, Lord.
Heal us please!
We who suffer
from disease.

But if a soul
can there, be saved,
give what
Anne Marie displays.

Strength.

Fathers

Steeped in all the "could he"—
Questioned in the "would he"—
Followed by a "should he"—
A father takes the call.

In haste or fear,
or more severe,
it's here,
the walking, crawl.

The highest mountain holds no fear,
like what befalls a man,
the moment he first comes to feel
his child's newborn hand.

The father knows that all the world
is wicked to its core.
And, how he'll guide his newfound pride
he soon starts to explore.

Fortunate is *he*—
Who brings his fear unto the Lord.

After all, no shoulder's carried
what His has, before.

And when the Lord receives that prayer,
He orders future steps.

No guarantees of ease,
but a forgiveness of our debts.

We tend to wreck what's precious—
We tend to break what's new—

We tend to do the very things
that *fathers* shouldn't do.

But deep in imperfection
is forgiveness for the one,

who humbles all he is
before another Father's Son.

And deep within His council,
be assured that you will learn . . .

Father is a name
that's not given, only earned.

Father's

The weight a child carries
is the weight we bequeath.
A child is refined
in the content we teach.

A child will reflect
what their parent projects.
If the parent should neglect,
then the child rejects.

And what comes about
is a problem for all.
A million missed chances
to teach while they crawl.

And once they grow tall,
their eyes see it all.
Replaying the pain
and the evil they saw.

A weed has now grown
unchecked in their heart.
The roots they protrude
tearing innocence apart.

A thirst for the nurture,
reduced them to nature,
where children; born givers,
are forced to be takers.

No faith in a maker
that's made His appeal.
Too afraid of the pain
when the cost is revealed.

The hate that they carry
is the weight they then give.
Forcing us all
to live how they lived.

But remember that child
that first was refused?
They were loved by the Lord
well before the abuse.

And a father that chooses
to hurt those God loves,
will incur the judgement
of what his seed does.

The Girl I Know

She stares, no care is in her.
The window draws her view.

She looks out at the world
filled with hope in what is true.

Her tiny, gentle person . . .
The warmth of her embrace.

Her smile ignites the room,
if you prove worthy of that face.

Her youth, it shows the hope she holds
for all her eyes can see.

But many years from now
she will endure what shouldn't be.

Truth she'll find, alludes a few
and in its place, abuse.

Where innocence itself
is quickly shattered through this view.

The things we show our children
aren't the things our Father shows.

They come from darkened places
where the wicked hide their souls.

But often times the hurting
are so hurt they fail to see.

The hurt they choose to carry
is the curse they then bequeath.

And when her gentle eyes
beheld the sight of painful hurt,

she was forced to grow much older.
But a boldness there, would stir.

And though her youth was stolen
what replaced it would ensure,

that she was far too powerful
to own another's curse.

If you can't remember the date,
If you can't remember the time,
If you can't remember the moment,
Stop everything and say these words...

Jesus, I believe YOU are the Son of God,
that YOU died on the cross to rescue me
from sin and death and to restore me to the
Father. I choose now to turn from my sins,
my self-centeredness, and every part of my
life that does not please YOU. I choose
YOU. I give myself to YOU.

Don't ASSUME your salvation,

ASSURE it!